Build *It* With Baby Steps

Kelly Crews

Build *It* With Baby Steps

Copyright © 2019 by Kelly Crews.

All rights reserved. No part of this book may be reproduced in any form or by any electronic or mechanical means, including information storage and retrieval systems, without permission in writing from the author, except by a reviewer who may quote brief passages in a review.

Printed in the United States of America

ISBN: 978-1-64633-248-9

Copyright, Legal Notice and Disclaimer:

Please note that much of this publication is based on educational research, personal experience, and anecdotal evidence. Although the author and publisher have made every reasonable attempt to achieve complete accuracy of the content in this book, they assume no responsibility for errors or omissions.

Any trademarks, service marks, product names, or named features are assumed to be the property of their respective owners and are used only for reference. There is no implied endorsement if we use one of these terms.

Build *It* With Baby Steps

Table of Contents

Endorsements- 5

Foreword- 7

Introduction- 11

Chapter One- *Where Do I Start?* 17

Chapter Two- *Make It All Work For You* 39

Chapter Three- *Stop Being So Hard On Yourself And Do It* 48

Chapter Four- *Small Budget Or No Budget... No Excuses* 62

Chapter Five- *Stick To Your Plan* 89

Endorsements

Build IT With Baby Steps is truly a transformational read. Kelly Crews inspires you to quit procrastinating; while also providing you with practical steps to execute your vision and start living the life of your dreams. She carries a wealth of wisdom and since following her guidance, my life hasn't been the same.

Cecily Nobles- Owner of 29E11

If you have dreams that have not become a reality, then this book is the missing piece to the puzzle. This book makes you rethink your purpose or passion and propels you to take steps to birth greatness.

Kelly Crews has written a must-read manuscript that will catapult you into reaching your destiny. Read this book and learn from the best!

Shaletha Sanders- www.shalethasander.org

Foreword

Every progressive leader across this nation and the world has had a moment during the course of their lives where their vision has kept them up late at night or they've gotten lost in their thoughts daydreaming about how to make their vision become a reality. When faced with what can easily feel overwhelming and frightening... there are always four simple words that enter into their hearts and minds.... "Where do I start?" Every leader, author, designer, minister, athlete, speaker, educator, entrepreneur, or CEO have all thought about these four words. No matter the vision or specific path that it leads you on...

knowing where to start is the first huge step that must be taken in order to manifest the vision that you so desire to see in the world.

In "Build It with Baby Steps" Kelly Crews provides an incredible way of helping leaders and visionaries, regardless of their level influence, begin to take practical, daily steps to answer the question of "Where do I start?" She challenges the reader to overcome the fear of launching out for the first time or to go back and pick up a vision that may have run into a brick wall and try it again! Kelly pushes the reader to move outside of thoughts that only lead to procrastination and disappointment to a life of strategy and productivity that will inevitably lead to confidence, momentum and success!

"Build It with Baby Steps" is filled with tools for the reader to write down their vision and goals so that they can remain accountable to the process of manifesting their vision. This book takes when can appear to be a massive vision and breaks it down into baby steps so that the reader can create a daily strategy to execute, execute, execute! Kelly understands that life happens and we can easily get discouraged in the process of launching out and offers affirmations that will easily help to encourage and inspire the reader as they continue on their journey or bringing their vision to fruition!

Every leader and visionary should keep this book in their collection of phenomenal reads! When faced with a massive vision that seems daunting and overwhelming, "Build It with Baby Steps" will push, challenge, encourage, motivate and inspire them to overcome fear and any trepidation as they move their vision forward!

Karri Turner, M.Div. -www.karriturner.org

Introduction

If you are waiting for a sign, consider this it. Life is so precious and so many people live from the shoreline or sideline looking out. They are dreaming, but never actualize the dream into reality. I don't like the words potential and aspiring. They leave room for probability, possibility and *IT* prospectively happening in the future. But, what about the purpose that you have now? Every single person has greatness within them, waiting to come out. It is a matter of knowing what you are passionate about. The problem is that we may know our passion and vision but get stuck trying to launch it. If you can't get started on a project or are stuck somewhere along the way, baby steps to success can be your answer that will finally set you in motion. We get stuck for all sorts of reasons, whether we realize it or not. It generally boils down to being afraid, overwhelmed, intimidated, uncomfortable, or insecure. Also, often, we get stuck financially. You don't see the finances of how to complete it, so out of frustration, you just don't start at all.

Taking baby steps can help you move forward when nothing else can. You can't build your entire vision in 24 hours, 1 week or 1 month. 6 months is a possibility, if you have all the money, components, the *right* people and the tenacity to finish. This is still a stretch. As the saying goes, "Rome wasn't built in a day." Rushing, cutting corners, waiting on people to do what they said they were going to do for you with a motive and building wrong can cause you to have a faulty foundation. So, relax! Take your time and build a vision that will last and give you influence.

Why does taking a baby step work?

No matter what kind of big success you want to achieve in life or how much money you want to earn from your business, you can accomplish your goals with baby steps.

A lot of people fail to realize that baby steps are the ones responsible for their success.

They want to make it big, but they don't want to start small, which is why they fail.

Baby steps help us to avoid all that because a baby step is so small and easy that it doesn't trigger fear, the pressure to perform, anxiety or discomfort. A well-designed baby step is easy *for you,* where you are right now. It's something that you can do effortlessly. It's just a teeny-tiny step from where you are. It's simple, discrete, and not intimidating.

Maybe you won't get miraculous results in a week or thirty days, but you can see substantial progress in six months, even if the steps you're taking seem small and inconsequential. They will add up over time.

While some people can just knock it out with sheer determination and will-power, the rest of us regular folk need to inch our way, day by day, in the direction of our ultimate objective. When consistently executed, those baby-steps will eventually lead to hard-core transformation and proven results.

And because you're taking steps that are easy for you, you'll be able to sustain your activity over those six to twelve months or a lifetime. The next thing you know is that you have completed what you wanted to accomplish for so long.

"Great visions are built by a series of small accomplishments that are effectively brought together and executed to completion."

Unknown

CHAPTER ONE

Where Do I Start?

Think you're not ready yet? Think again! All the best intentions, talk, and magazine articles in the world won't change your life unless you actually have that "I-can-totally-do-this" kind of moment and push yourself into high gear. We often think there will be this spotlight from the sky event illuminating the exact right moment when we should get started on a journey toward our goals. But let me tell you, that "I'll start on Monday mentality" might keep you from ever getting where you need to go. Planning, planning, planning (yeah, like procrastinating) but never executing, if this is you, this is your time to make it happen.

You want to open a business, write a book, start a ministry, launch a social platform, become a life coach, be an activist, have a global, online store or build your brand. But where do you start? You can see the big picture but have no idea where to begin. There is planning to do, from business registration, incorporation, getting a tax ID, designing a website, marketing, launching, social media and business card creation, advertising, creating clientele to whatever else could be on this endless and overwhelming list. This, in itself, is mind-boggling to someone who is just beginning or maybe you are starting over.

Let's face it, most people desire financial freedom, want to be successful and want to embrace their destiny. But, the problem is that it takes time and effort. We hear about getting rich quick schemes and social media has many people fooled into thinking everything is easy. That person with 1 million followers may be in a worse position than you are. It just appears that they have their life together. They may have the same thought of "where do I start?"

There is no way that you can skip the process and get to the destination in one step. But, this does not mean that you have to struggle and go through a lot of pain as so often taught. No matter what kind of big success you want to achieve in life or how much money you want to earn from your business, you need to start with baby steps. A lot of people fail to realize that baby steps are the ones responsible for their success. They want to make it big, but they don't want to start small, which is why they fail.

Every big success was once started small. Every master was once a beginner. Think of this principle.

Before you can reap, you must sow. However, many people want to reap before they sow.

Babies learn to walk before they run. So what makes you think you can skip the process to get the success you want? There are so many main-stream multi-million and billion dollars companies that started with an idea in a garage. I am talking about Apple, Google, Amazon and I know there are so many more!

No matter what it is that you want to accomplish, start small. Take one small step at a time. This will ensure that you are doing it right and you will get to where you want to go!

Here's why taking baby steps are important to your success.

1. It gives you clarity and focus

Success requires clarity and focus. And without the focus on where you want to go, you will feel lost and get overwhelmed with information overload.

When you start with baby steps, you will know exactly what you need to do. And all you have to do is to follow the steps.

You don't really worry or care about what is going to happen in the next 10 years, all you do is focus on the current progress and do what is required now.

2. It prevents procrastination

How many of us are guilty of this, including me! People procrastinate and delay getting their work done because they feel overwhelmed mentally, emotionally and spiritually.

They feel that the work or vision is too big to handle and they have no idea where to start. Sometimes, thinking of the overall cost of a vision can stagnate you and make you procrastinate. We think, "I can't do it now, because I don't have the money or I will wait until I am in a better financial position." We can even put things on hold until that "person" comes to bless us. You could be waiting years for some phenomenon to happen in your life and you waste valuable time that could have been used to execute the plan God gave to you. Stop overthinking what you know you are supposed to do. Putting off until tomorrow what you can do today is a conscious decision.

Like many decisions, emotions are involved, whether or not you are aware. When you procrastinate, you may have more than a productivity problem. You could also have an emotional obstacle in the way of your success. When you are emotionally exhausted or drained, it is difficult to function properly, so we tend to put off what needs to be done. But, I want you to begin to ask God to help you regulate your emotions and give you the strength to accomplish even if, "you don't feel like it." Refusing to do what you don't feel like doing is a maturity issue. In order to succeed, you HAVE to do it.

Past disappointments will cause people to procrastinate. If you've been disappointed in life over and over and over, you learn to expect more of the same.

Succeeding requires effort to go where you want to go in life. You may procrastinate the work involved because you've learned that "nothing works out as planned anyway."

This is your old disappointment talking. It's trying to protect you from the pain of further disappointment. If you decide ahead of time that you'll never get what you want, then why bother trying? You're basically saying, "*I'll take my disappointment now, rather than wait until later. I will save myself from doing a ton of pointless work."*

Unfortunately, protection from disappointment guarantees you'll be disappointed, forever. The only way to experience the joy of accomplishment is to risk the disappointment of failure. If you work smart and take baby steps, you have a great chance of succeeding.

In many cases, you are guaranteed success if you put in the effort. If you can escape that self-inflicted battle with disappointment, You can learn to enjoy the joy of productivity and success.

3. It builds your confidence and grows your momentum

One of the main reasons successful people are able to produce amazing results is that they have the momentum and confidence.

And it all comes from taking one small step at a time. When you accomplish one small step, you create one small victory that will boost your self-confidence.

The more small wins you create, the more confident you become. Celebrating small wins is an important way to track incremental achievements and work toward much larger goals. Plus, it makes you feel good more often.

In a study of how everyday life inside organizations can influence a person's performance, researchers analyzed nearly 12,000 diary entries from 238 employees across seven companies.

They found that capturing small wins every day enhances a worker's motivation. Simply recording progress in some way helps to boost self-confidence and can be put to use toward future successes. There is science behind this thought process too. When you accomplish something, it activates the reward center of our brains, allowing us to feel a sense of pride. Specifically, the neurochemical dopamine is released and it energizes us. This chemical helps you to experience the feeling of getting rewarded and can leave you with wanting to achieve even more.

These modest behavior changes set off a positive chain reaction for even bigger developments later on. Even if they take just 5 to 10 minutes, small wins can stack up over time and become significant markers of progress and happiness.

4. It lowers your resistance to begin

The bigger the task, the more time and energy it is going to take. But when it comes to baby steps, it is easier to get done. And this actually lowers your resistance to begin and to get it done.

So, the next time when you feel you don't have the motivation to do the task, break it down further into even smaller pieces, and then just start. It is not too big for you to accomplish. God gave it to you. He knows what you will need along the way and you are simply responsible for moving forward with the plan. There is no way around it. You can't skip the steps.

You can't lose 10 pounds straight after your first exercise session. Of course, that would be amazing, but it takes discipline. It all starts small and the results will accumulate.

Hence, stop buying into the idea that you can lose weight, earn big money, or build a successful business, brand or ministry without putting in the work.

Let me help you get started, TODAY!

My Someday Goal

What is the one thing you want to do someday?

_____

_____

_____

_____

_____

_____

_____

My Five-year Goal

Based on your someday goal, what's the one thing you can do in the next five years?

_____

_____

_____

_____

_____

_____

_____

_____

_____

_____

Build *It* With Baby Steps

My One-year Goal

Based on your five-year goal, what's the one thing you can do this year?

_____

_____

_____

_____

_____

_____

_____

_____

_____

_____

My Monthly Goal

Based on your one-year your goal, what's the one thing you can do this month?

_____

_____

_____

_____

_____

_____

_____

_____

_____

Build *It* With Baby Steps

My Weekly Goal

Based on your monthly goal, what's the one thing you can do this week?

_____

_____

_____

_____

_____

_____

_____

_____

_____

_____

My Daily Goal

Based on your weekly goal, what's the one thing you can do today?

_____

_____

_____

_____

_____

_____

_____

_____

_____

_____

Build *It* With Baby Steps

My Right Now Goal

Based on your daily goal, what's the one thing you can do right now?

_____

_____

_____

_____

_____

_____

_____

_____

_____

Congratulations, you've just officially taken your first baby step!

"What's the point of being alive if you don't at least try to do something remarkable?"

Unknown

CHAPTER TWO

Make It All Work For You

Now that you understand the importance of taking baby steps, let's talk about how you can begin to make it all work for you. As you just learned in the exercise in Chapter One, the easiest way to apply the concept of taking baby steps is to break down your bigger tasks into smaller ones.

For example, if you need to create an article for your blog, you can break this task into many smaller pieces such as:

- Create the article title

- Draft the subheadings

- Write the first 1,000 words. Sometimes, sitting down in front of a computer or writing can be intimidating, so try this. Voice record your thoughts and transcribe them into your concept. This can be very helpful when you have writer's block.

- Write the second 1,000 words, or complete the article

- Spell and grammar check and proofread

- Insert relevant links and images

- Publish the article

As you can see, the one task, to write and publish an article on your blog has now been broken down into many smaller pieces that you can manage easily. When you do this, you are greatly lowering the resistance of the bigger task and make it easy to do. The steps become clear and you know what you need to accomplish.

Another method you can use is to limit the time that you spend on a task. Stop killing yourself. Think about it like this. You don't have to work out in the gym for 2 hours straight. Most people can't make it for more than 30 minutes. All you need to do is to commit to working out in moderation.

Find an effective workout and eating plan that will get you RESULTS! Give yourself *windows of time* to complete one goal.

For instance, when you think about being at the gym for 2 hours, it can seem like a daunting and exhausting task. But, you can challenge yourself, when you give yourself 10 or 15-minute increments to complete a portion of the workout. Now, anyone can finish a 10-minute exercise. The key is to limit the time frame and to put yourself into action. When you are in motion, you will build up momentum and you will want to continue in steps until you are finished.

Here are a few reasons why you may want to embrace this mindset. When you're more organized and time conscious, there's no doubt you tend to be more successful in life and business. If success is your ultimate goal (which I assume it is), you will begin to focus on completing those important tasks that will boost your business and give you the results you deserve. When you start doing it, not only today, but right now, this will stop you from procrastinating. It might not be the cure-all you're seeking, but it can certainly change the way you view your workload and get through your workday.

Excuses are easy to find, so why not challenge yourself to get up out of your chair and do a few small tasks? The reality is you have nothing to lose.

There are a lot of little tasks that are well-worth a nod of accomplishment despite their seeming insignificance in the grand scheme of things. Over the span of a week, or even a month, those mini-moments of satisfaction can leave you feeling pretty accomplished every day. Even when you're having a bad day, you owe it to yourself to acknowledge your efforts, no matter how small.

One of the best things that can occur from this whole practice is the fact that you are seemingly making executive decisions without even realizing it. You're putting action behind things and minimizing the need to second guess everything. There's no unnecessary thoughtful contemplation or deliberation. You can focus on finishing.

I challenge you to try this for yourself. This simple strategy can really change the way you handle productivity. Some people believe that productivity is about cramming everything they can into each day. It's not. Productivity is about making progress that lasts. Here are some synonyms of productivity: fruitfulness, productiveness, prolificacy, prolificity, cleverness, creativeness, creativity, imagination, imaginativeness, ingeniousness, ingenuity, innovativeness, invention, inventiveness, originality, capableness and resourcefulness.

It's incredible to see that just by introducing one tiny habit into your life, you can make immense changes.

"An inch of movement will bring you closer to your goals than a mile of intention."

Steve Maraboli

CHAPTER THREE

Stop Being So Hard On Yourself And Do It

We all live each day with our own hang-ups and issues. Sure, we'd like to believe that every last thing we accomplish is done with complete confidence and ease, but that would ignore the fact that life is filled with an amazing number of challenges, shifts, changes, let-downs and surprises. Sometimes, "just" showing up means you're accomplishing something pretty amazing.

Sometimes, just keeping the idea or vision in front of you is all you can do for that particular day.

But, I have a little reminder for you. You are stronger than you think. As we go through life, challenges arise to help us keep growing. We're human and we have layers. Just when we think we've learned something, life comes along and shows us there's more.

Anyone who's ever faced a major hurdle and found themselves quick on their feet, anyone who's taken on an unbelievable upset with grace and anyone who's sacrificed their comfort for vision knows this. When you take on something really big, you find strengths you never imagined you had. Connecting to your authentic self and finding purpose is going to challenge you to grow.

So, you have to stop being so hard on yourself. To stop being too hard on yourself, it's important to be reasonable and treat *yourself* with respect. Empower yourself to make your life better rather than wasting your energy beating yourself up. You are not stupid or dumb, because you didn't do x, y and z two years ago. Stop focusing on the past and what you could've or should've done and start making progress in your present. In those moments, it's easy to panic, especially if you start to over analyze or overthink. You have to have realistic expectations! You may have had to make mistakes to learn and grow from them. Embrace your vision journey and commit to learning and self-improvement to be the best you can be. There are people on this earth waiting for what you have to offer. Someone is waiting for you to show up. Focus your efforts on those things you can change. Maybe a few things went wrong in the past but look for the lessons and stop attacking your mind, heart and spirit over it.

It's easy to look at others and compare your own path to theirs. But, the danger lies in that you can start thinking that you are never going to be successful like "them, never get to that platform or never have the right connections. Stop comparing yourself to random people on social media or strangers on the internet. I saw a statistic that stated that 7 out of 10 people on Instagram do not have at least $1000.00 in their bank account. Also, I read an article about a young lady who was considered an influencer with 1.2 million followers on Instagram. She launched a t-shirt line and only sold 36 t-shirts. Can you imagine? We have to stop looking at people and gauging the number of followers as the definition of success. Someone may look "popular," but that does not mean that they have genuine influence. Influence leaves a legacy. Influence has staying power. You are not looking for 15 minutes of fame. You want your vision to outlast you. Influence reaches the audience that you intend to reach. It may take time, but it will be worth it.

Oh, and then we have the critics and unwanted advisors who can really kill your spirit when it comes to your vision. Some criticism can be justified at times. However, it's important to keep it constructive and in perspective. Make sure that you are not overwhelmed by people's opinions that are not conducive to your growth. You don't have to share everything with everybody. Don't let the whole world know your plans as you are building. Some people are literally assigned to sabotage your plans and talk you out of your destiny. If you let them, by the time they get done with you, you will want to give up and do nothing. Stop letting people make you feel bad for having a vision that you are actually going to see manifest. Let's be honest, it is a bit disappointing and can make you feel sad when someone doesn't support you, your product, business idea or style, but you have to rise above your emotions. There are always going to be people that are not for you. But, you don't have to let them dull your shine. Honestly, they are a smaller percentage of people than you think. You will never be able to please everyone all the time and make them love everything you do. It is impossible. So, focus on the 99 % that will and forget about that 1%. Keep your focus. You need to have people around you that are true supporters.

I am not talking about "yes people." I am talking about people who love, respect or like you enough to be honest with you and push you further by celebrating your achievements.

Ok, who has those annoying voices inside their head that question everything you do and the brilliant ideas you come up with? I saw a lot of hands go up. They're called "the negative committee" because all they do is work against your will to win.

It is so imperative that you don't become your own enemy or worst critic. Your thoughts and words matter and negative thoughts and words distort your reality. There's nothing to be gained from criticizing yourself over and over again. It's a waste of time, it's disempowering and it will keep you stuck.

So, try this. Whenever you have those inner doubts and you find yourself thinking, "I can't do this because...," tell the thoughts to shut up! Silence the sound that no one else hears but you. You will be instantly empowered and feel in control again.

I want you to embrace these points as you are building with baby steps. Every day may not be the "best" day of your life, but you can make it what you want it to be. You can run the day or let the day run you. Do it now, because, "I will do it later" becomes never. Don't put *IT* off anymore!

Focus on the positives

There are always positives. However, you probably won't see them when you're too hard on yourself. You will have to make a conscious effort to see them. Ask yourself what you've done well, and the things that you like about yourself and your life.

Write down 5 things that you like about yourself...

_____

_____

_____

_____

_____

Use affirmations

For example, "I am not perfect, but I am learning and growing." Or, "I have the power to create the life I desire and deserve." "God has a plan for me and I am going to fulfill it."

Create your own affirmations...

_____

_____

_____

_____

_____

Treat yourself great

Be kind to yourself and love who you are and what you are doing. Give yourself permission to try things out and find a passion for the process. Nurture yourself as a person and truly see your overall worth.

I am worthy to do this because...

_____

_____

_____

_____

I give myself permission to...

_____

_____

_____

_____

_____

_____

I'd rather look back at my life and say, "I can't believe I did that," instead of saying, " I wish I would've done that."

Unknown

CHAPTER FOUR

Small Budget Or No Budget...No Excuses

Most people do not have a cool million in their bank account to play around with. In fact, many entrepreneurs will have some of the greatest ideas, but no capital to invest in their vision. But, this doesn't excuse you from starting. So many people think that they have to "wait" until they have their finances in order or have thousands of dollars saved to launch their God-given idea. Not so. Nearly every small business owner has stories to share about how they started out on a shoestring budget and managed to survive their first years by being creative with limited cash. If you're one of those entrepreneurs who want to know how to grow your small business on a budget, there's hope.

Every great business or vision starts with drive and a passion. Moguls like Richard Branson, Oprah, Bill Gates, Tyler Perry and Warren Buffett started at zero. Lack of funds should not deter you from pursuing your entrepreneurial dreams. With confidence in your idea and a clear vision of how you are going to execute it, you can do it.

There are tens of millions of small businesses, in whatever category, in the United States alone, and starting a new business to compete in this segment will require hard work and dedication. Being practical is extremely important when you are taking baby steps to start your vision or idea. You need a steady source of income before you can set up your business, so it's advisable to hold onto your current job. By retaining your present job, you will be more secure when you need to take make small investments into what you are launching. I love hearing people say that they are working to fund their vision and when the time is right, they will leave their job. This is wisdom to the highest degree. I worked two jobs, at one point, while I was traveling and preaching. Sometimes, I was working 24-hour shifts. I knew that the small investments that I could make at the time would pay off in the long-run.

You will, of course, need to spend extra hours and work harder, but that's what the baby steps are for. Improvising your small business through these lean years might seem unappealing and frustrating at times, but by using some of the tools I am going to give you here, you'll soon see your small business start to grow. In the early stages of business or ministry, when the budget is lean, you have to find creative ways to operate with a small team or even no team at all and still get the job done. Sometimes, as you are beginning, it is better to do it yourself, instead of trying to implement a "team."

Ask yourself what you can do and get for free or with very little investment.

It's easy to come up with a list of obstacles standing in the way of you and launching your business. It's often harder to come up with a list of opportunities that are right in front of you. If the thought of starting a business with no money scares you, stop and reflect on what you can do without right now.

What's essential to your business or ministry? If you do things properly in the beginning, you won't have to backtrack. Some of you may say,

"I am already established or semi-established, but I am not getting the results I want. This may be the right time to rework your vision, rebrand and relaunch. If you have the components in place, you will be able to build the visibility, networking opportunities and clientele you are looking for.

You have to develop your area of expertise. Before you can establish or develop your expertise, you have to decide what you want to be known for. The world of personal branding is flooded, so it isn't enough to be general. Instead, it's best to develop yourself in a very specific niche. With a niche focus, you'll have more opportunities to prove you know what you're talking about or your product/s value, and while your potential audience might be slightly smaller, you will also be that much more relevant.

The following is a list of what every entrepreneur needs to begin or add successfully and build credibility.

1. A website
2. Social media- Facebook, Instagram and Twitter
3. A mission and vision statement
4. A bio
5. A logo
6. Professional photos- if you are a public speaker of any kind
7. Appealing photos of your product/s

8. Inviting videos/ YouTube

9. Register your business name

10. Get a tax identification number- EIN with the IRS (in the United States)

11. Register your business or non-profit with the state or country you live in.

12. For a non-profit or incorporation, create your articles of incorporation and bylaws

13. Set up a business bank account

14. Set up a business PayPal or Square account to take online payments and donations, or you may also use resources like Venmo and the CashApp.

Don't have a panic attack! This is going to cost you less than you think! There are a ton of free and VERY inexpensive tools online that can help you grow your business, as well as free trials available for online products that will simplify your building and marketing processes.

Here are some that you can start using right away and before you know it, your baby steps will have a big payoff.

***Fiverr.com*-** literally has tons of website, logo and graphic designers, creators, editors, influencers and pretty much anything you need to outsource your project to for near pennies! This is an amazing online source for anyone on a budget.

Canva.com, Designbold.com & Pablo- will give you the look of professionally designed graphics for your blog, website, social media, YouTube channel or marketing materials without the cost or the expertise. These companies will be your new best friend. Use pre-formatted templates to create social media banners, blog graphics, marketing flyers, and much more. Free and extremely easy to use, they will take your amateur, no-budget marketing effort and make you look like a seasoned pro or that you paid a top designer to create it. Your Facebook and Twitter pages should have professional looking banners to represent you. You can make those with these design companies.

Mailchimp.com - will allow you to create and send creative email announcements for marketing and networking purposes.

Hootsuite.com and the Planoly App for Instagram - Publishing individual social media messages in real-time is a drain on time. By signing up for Hootsuite, you can manage multiple social profiles from a single dashboard. Schedule posts, track mentions, engage with followers, and measure the effectiveness of your social media content, at no cost. It's the go-to tool for keeping your social media accounts in line.

PayPal.com and Square.com - business services allow you to invoice new clients and accept credit card payment on your website or by the app on your phone. It takes less than 10 minutes to set up and boom, you can take your first payment!

Venmo.com, Zelle.com and the CashApp - are great ways to also take payments or donations.

Grammerly.com - writing app makes sure everything you type is easy to read, effective, and mistake-free. Grammarly automatically detects grammar, spelling, punctuation, word choice and style mistakes in your writing.

Apps that are great for putting text on your social media posts include: Studio for iPhone, Typorama, Word Swag, ReType, Adobe Spark Post and WordDream. You want your social media to look great and when you add your own text, you can add your website too.

***Formswift.com*-** is perfect for your articles of incorporation and bylaws. You don't have to pay someone $500- $1000 to complete your paperwork for you. This is about a 10-minute process. You select a template from the library of 500+ documents. Then fill out a step-by-step questionnaire and export your completed document in Word or PDF. It is simple and painless.

Pixabay.com, Flickr.com & Freeimages.com- Beautiful images are essential to making your vision, business or ministry stand out online. But if you're not a professional photographer and your product isn't visually compelling, how can you use images in your marketing effort? Try these free stock images site to search for images to use in your blog, social media, and other marketing materials.

Facebook and Instagram Live and Periscope- are great ways to start building a major following. If you are bold, organized and present yourself or product properly, you will be surprised at the response that live videos receive.

***www.zoom.us*-** is a company that provides remote conferencing services using cloud computing. Zoom offers communications software that combines video conferencing, online meetings, chat, and mobile collaboration. You can have a virtual training or conference. You can do mentoring and coaching!

If you know your audience and focus, it is time to put the action behind your plan. To move ahead, you've got to get started. You can either continue to think about, talk about, and dream about your goals, or you can actually start (like right this minute) on your way to making it happen. You're one decision away from a totally better and different life. Trust me, you're ready right now. Now, get to it!

So, finally, let's talk about the "M" word. Money! Some of you are still concerned about your finances. Don't be, because you are going to put yourself on a budget that will make sense, so you take the financial pressure off of yourself when it comes to your business plan. Learn to be flexible. In your first year of budgeting, you may have to make a lot of adjustments, but that's OK. Here are a few larger ticket things that will be an investment but are necessary and very worth it. I am only listing the basics.

Website- $100 - $600 (for a *nice* site and yes, you can have an awesome website for less than you think.)

State business registration- $70 -$150

Professional photos- $200 - $400 (for good ones)

Passport- $125 (If you want to travel internationally and this is for the United States)

Boosting your Facebook post- $5 - $500 (just depends on what you choose.)

Ok, so when you add this up, you are looking at close to $1000 or more. I want to make this simple for you.

While you are taking your baby steps and getting your vision in order, you can be saving towards one of the items on this list. You don't have to do everything at one-time. You are budgeting and balancing at the same time. I know you are balancing all of your other expenses too, but each time you are able to save and pay off one of these items, you will feel amazing! It is the same thing with your debt.

Someone is saying, "How do I do this?" Well, think about all the fast food, Starbucks, Duncan Donuts, Target and Walmart runs you make a week. You can go to Target for one small thing and before you know it, you walk out spending $50.00. By cutting back on all the unnecessary little things you buy each day, you will be surprised by what you have left at the end of one week. Challenge yourself not to buy stuff that you don't need. Instead of a Venti Caramel Macchiato at Starbucks, get a regular cup of coffee. I know it's not as exciting and not what you really wanted, but you still get your coffee and you save about $4.00. Or, better yet, make coffee at home before you leave. It is free!

Don't go out to eat on your lunch break every day or buy something for dinner every evening. You will spend $10.00 alone at Panera or Chipotle every single time.

If you add up everything you are spending on random food and drinks every week, you will be shocked. Let me give you an example. If you are spending $15 a day on food, it adds up to $105 a week and $420 a month. You already have more money than you think you do. Then, let's add $100 a month from the different stores, when you go to "grab" a few things. Now, you have spent $520 and you can't account for it.

Stop yourself. Make a very strict list when you go shopping or to the grocery store and stick to it. Make yourself lunch and dinner. Have more discipline when it comes to spending. Before you know it, you will have saved up enough money to begin to implement your plans and purchase the necessities to truly launch or relaunch your business, brand, or ministry.

I challenge you to do this for 30 days and see what happens. This challenge entails making changes to your daily habits. The point is to challenge yourself and see how far you can stretch! A month can be really difficult, but the longer the challenge, the greater the reward. If you're worried about how difficult it might be, start off easier with a no-spend weekend or week. At the end of the day, you have to ask yourself if you are really committed to your vision. How bad do you want this?

Build *It* With Baby Steps

Keep track of what you save for 30 days.

Week One

Weekly Planner

MON	
TUE	
WED	
THU	
FRI	
SAT	
SUN	

Week Two

Weekly Planner

MON	
TUE	
WED	
THU	
FRI	
SAT	
SUN	

Build *It* With Baby Steps

Week Three

Weekly Planner

MON	
TUE	
WED	
THU	
FRI	
SAT	
SUN	

Week Four

Weekly Planner

MON	
TUE	
WED	
THU	
FRI	
SAT	
SUN	

Once again, these baby are paying off big time! Congratulations on taking a major step in the right direction, even if it seems simple and small. What you couldn't see before will start to become clear to you. You don't have any excuses left. Tell yourself, *"Hey, _____, you can afford this."* That opens up your mind to think creatively and you will find ways and begin to feel empowered by catering to your desire to succeed.

> **"You can have it all.
> Just not all at once."**
> **Oprah**

CHAPTER FIVE

Stick To Your Plan

It feels great to create a plan that has smart baby steps and goals to meet. The challenge comes in following a plan to make those goals a reality. During the initial days of setting a goal, enthusiasm drives motivation to achieve results, but it isn't long before life happens and the goal can become overwhelming. It happens to everyone. Your happiest moments dissipate, and you have little or no energy to work creatively and enthusiastically. You feel mentally and emotionally drained. All your excitement about accomplishing your dreams, working on a project and achieving your financial goal, starting the business in which you have invested time, energy and finances is suddenly gone. You can't understand it or explain it. But there is one thing you are certain of, you may at times feel exhausted and you want your passion back!

While it's easy to embark on the pursuit of a worthwhile goal, the ability to maintain the momentum to ensure its accomplishment is another issue altogether. When your motivation is low, your commitment, determination and passion are tested. You become aware that your worthwhile goal will remain just that, unless you get motivated and stay motivated to achieve it.

Despite having lost the motivation to work on your most important goal, chances are you remain actively engaged in accomplishing other unrelated goals. However, despite these accomplishments, you continue to feel dissatisfied and unfulfilled, because your most worthy goal remains untouched, unattended to and unattained.

Motivation is the energy that drives you to accomplish goals, and it's necessary for all types of success. You need motivation in huge doses and you need it daily. Parents have to stay motivated to raise their kids. Students have to stay motivated to graduate from college and employees have to stay motivated to get promoted (and to stay employed).

Writers have to stay motivated to complete books, and business owners must stay motivated to make profits. Often, after the initial euphoria of achieving one goal has waned, you need the motivation to begin working on the next goal. Motivation is the energy that keeps you trying one more time, when everything around you says give up.

Research suggests that less than 10 percent of people feel they achieve their goals. That means 90 percent don't, which is a staggering number.

The question is, what do the 10 percent do that the 90 percent don't?

There are many factors that go into whether or not goals are reached, but two important components are **1)** a strategic plan, and **2)** commitment to work the plan. Even when you are totally psyched up about achieving a goal, your motivation can be affected by several factors, including disappointment in others, the loss of a loved one, hitting a plateau after a huge accomplishment, becoming overwhelmed, and failure to reap immediate rewards for your hard work. Further, the condition of your personal surroundings, fear, personal insecurities, unhealthy relationships that sap your positive energy, current projects, and even fatigue can drain valuable motivation.

The first thing to do when you've lost your motivation is to face the situation, confront it and then correct it. When a car you rely on to get to work every day won't start, you do everything within your power to have the problem fixed. You do this because the reward of having your car in good condition is worth the effort it takes to repair it. In the same way, when the motivation you rely on to accomplish a goal is gone, you must do everything within your power to rekindle the fire. You must remain focused on the desired end result. Focus on the freedom and reward you will gain as a result of achieving your goal.

Make a list of the reasons why you want to achieve this goal and why it is important to you. It can't just be money-motivated or you may become defeated before you begin.

It is really easy to get blown off course in our busy and distracting world. This is why it is vital to ground yourself in your goal. Write down the reasons why you want to achieve a particular goal and why it is so important to you. What drives you and where does your passion come from pertaining to your vision? Studies have shown that when we write by hand, manually connecting the letters, engages the brain more actively.

Why do I want to achieve this goal?

_____

_____

_____

Why is it important to me?

_____

_____

_____

All in all, you must have a strong answer to WHY you want to reach your goal, in order to stay motivated. So, get down to what really drives you and why you really want something. This way, you will be 100% committed.

It's both possible and necessary to regain lost motivation, and it's easier than you think! You can take simple steps to stay enthusiastic and committed every step of the way until you achieve your worthwhile goal.

Identify your greatest sources of inspiration and motivation.

- Grab a pen and notepad and write down the names of three people in whose presence you come alive or whose words inspire your faith and confidence?

- If you have a personal relationship with them, what was the last thing each of these people said to you that meant so much, and how can those words motivate you today?

- Get in touch with these three people this week. Call, email or visit each one and let them know that you appreciate them and the value they have brought to your life. Don't be afraid to ask for help in becoming motivated to achieve your goal. I have several people that I can explicitly trust and I can go to when I need prayer or motivation and this helps me tremendously!

When it comes to motivation, attitude is everything. Different people may have completely opposite feelings towards the same task. Some will hate it and others will love it. Why do you think this happens? It's simple. Some of us find ways to make any task interesting and fun to do!

Depending on how you look at it, you can have fun doing just about anything! Just look for ways of having fun, and you'll find them! A simple approach is to start working on any task by asking yourself a few questions:

- How can I enjoy this task?

- What can I do to make this task fun for myself and possibly for others?

- How can I make this work the best part of my day?

As long as you learn to have the definite expectation of any task being potentially enjoyable, you will start to feel motivated.

Some of you will probably think of a thing or two, which are valid exceptions from this statement, like something you always hate doing no matter how hard you try making it fun. You're probably right, and that's why I don't claim everything to be fun. However, most tasks have a great potential of being enjoyable, and so looking for ways to have fun while working is definitely a good habit to acquire.

When something doesn't feel right, it's always a good time to take a moment and look for a different approach for the task.

You may be doing everything correctly and most efficiently, but such an approach isn't necessarily the most motivating one. Quite often, you can find a number of obvious tweaks to your current approach, which will both change your experience and open up new possibilities.

That's why saying "one way or another" is so common — if you really want to accomplish your goal, there is always a way; and most likely, there's more than one way.

If a certain approach doesn't work for you, find another one, and keep trying until you find the one which will both keep you motivated and get you the desired results.

Some people think that trying a different approach means giving up. They take pride in being really stubborn and refusing to try any other options on their way towards the goal.

My opinion on this is that the power of focus is great, but you should be focusing on your goal, and not limiting your options by focusing on just one way to accomplish it.

We track our progress automatically with most activities. But to stay motivated, you need to *recognize* your progress, not merely track it. Tracking and recognizing your progress is different.

Tracking is merely taking note of having reached a certain stage in your process. I gave you a tracking chart in Chapter One. This is a great and necessary tool but recognizing is taking time to look at a bigger picture and realize where exactly you are, and how much more you have left to do.

Somehow, it is human nature always to want things to happen in the short term or even at once. Even though we split complex tasks into simpler actions, we don't quite feel the satisfaction until all is done and the task is fully complete.

For many scenarios, though, the task is so vast that such approach will drain all the motivation out of you long before you have a chance to reach your goal. That's why it is important to always take to baby steps and recognize the positive difference and progress made. This is how your motivation can sustain you in the long term.

Lastly, you have to reward yourself. Highly driven people often fail to pause and effectively acknowledge a job well done, especially smaller successes that are required on the road toward a big goal. Burnout, compromised personal life and health, and lost perspective can result.

Your reward does not have to involve spending. You can give yourself a block of time to watch a good movie or simply relax. You don't have to work 24/7/365. Take a breather, after each accomplishment to actually smell the roses for a moment. The more you reward yourself for the honestly made progress, the more motivated you will feel about reaching new milestones, thus finally accomplishing your goal. I am cheering for you and God wants you to win!

Jeremiah 29:11 says, "For I know the plans I have for you," declares the Lord, "plans to prosper you and not to harm you, plans to give you hope and a future."

Contact Kelly!

www.kellycrews.org

Twitter: @prophetesskelly

Facebook: @prophetesskelly

Instagram: @kellycrews

Do you need a mentor to push you in this area? Contact Kelly today.

kellycrewsglobal@gmail.com

www.ingramcontent.com/pod-product-compliance
Lightning Source LLC
LaVergne TN
LVHW011729060526
838200LV00051B/3083